M
Worshipping Mother

Reclaiming Mary's Motherhood for Contemporary Mums

Helen Collins

Tutor for Pastoral and Ministerial Studies,

Trinity College, Bristol

GROVE BOOKS LIMITED

RIDLEY HALL RD CAMBRIDGE CB3 9HU

Contents

Acknowledgments
With special thanks to my research participants for sharing their lives with me and to my children for inspiring the work.

First Impression December 2018
ISSN 0144-171X
ISBN 978 1 78827 069 4

1

Introduction

Am I the Only One Struggling?

I first experienced the charismatic renewal as a child and discovered a vibrant spirituality which nurtured me into young adulthood. However, after becoming a mother, I experienced a significant disconnection from these spiritual roots. Where previously I had regularly encountered God through charismatic forms of worship, as a mother I found I could no longer engage. Absorption in these previously fruitful spiritual practices felt impossible alongside constant care of a baby. I was continually taunted by the image of the ideal worshipper, perceived by me to be one who sings fervently, with both arms raised and eyes closed, utterly abandoned to the moment of intimate encounter with God, whilst I struggled to manage my needy infant, alone and isolated at the back of the church.

I began to feel that my spiritual life was inadequate and that I was to blame for this unwelcome change. If only I tried harder to engage, if only I was a better mother at settling my baby, then I too could rejoin the throng of faithful worshippers each Sunday. My transformation to motherhood seemed to have fundamentally and immediately changed my ability to relate to God in familiar and nourishing ways. I was completely unprepared for this change and seemed to lack the capacity to reflect on or process the changes. I also had no resources which could encourage or guide me through the difficulties. 'Cut adrift from a felt encounter with God and overwhelmed by the seemingly endless demands of new mothering, I felt confused, guilty, inadequate, frustrated, isolated and forgotten by God.'[1]

My transformation to motherhood seemed to have changed my ability to relate to God

Once the initial intensity of the baby phase began to subside, I was able to enter into sustained reflection upon the nature of these experiences. I wanted to know whether I was the only person who had ever felt like this. I began to question what might have caused these deep feelings of alienation and I wanted to know if there were ways to help other people having similar experiences. This personal quest for answers, and ultimately for reconciliation between my experiences and my much-cherished spiritual practices, slowly grew into a PhD where I carried out research into the spiritual lives of new mothers within the charismatic movement.[2] One of the surprising findings of the research was the potential Mary has to speak meaningfully to the situation of contemporary mothers.

This Grove booklet summarizes the findings of that research to show how Mary's story can be a significant source of pastoral care and support for new mothers struggling with church like I did. Whilst the research was carried out in the context of charismatic spirituality, I consider the findings to be of relevance to mothers of any church tradition who are struggling to engage in worship because of their mothering responsibilities. In addition, whilst the focus is on the experiences of new mothers, their struggles may similarly relate to other groups of people feeling alienated from worship practices because of their circumstances.

What Is the Problem?

My interviews with new mothers and my participant observation in charismatic churches revealed that most mothers find it difficult to engage with worship in church once they have a baby. A creche provision was common in the majority of the churches I observed, and whilst this served to enable them to be mothers in the space, it often did not succeed in facilitating their worship. The reasons for this tension between mothering and worship seemed to be twofold: first, it was due to an understanding of worship that placed the emphasis upon the worshipper's ability to engage; and secondly, because of contemporary understandings of mothering as intensive parenting. I shall outline these in turn.

A Process of Worship

In his 2006 study of the charismatic tradition, *Encountering the Spirit,* Mark Cartledge proposes a process and a framework of charismatic spirituality as a theological context for understanding the charismatic movement.[3] He conceives of charismatic spirituality as a cyclical process which moves from *search* to *encounter* to *transformation* and then back to *search*. This process can be applied to all forms of spirituality but he suggests that it is particularly helpful for understanding charismatic spirituality due to its distinctive concern for encountering the Holy Spirit and for a resulting personal transformation.

The process is initiated by means of a search for God, which for charismatics happens predominantly in praise and sung worship. During this search phase, the congregation are encouraged to transition from search for God into encounter with God. This is often demonstrated within charismatic churches by the transition from upbeat songs to more reflective, intimate songs. The encounter with God happens in this intimate singing and may also be experienced in prayer ministry. This in turn gives way to the third phase, where transformation is experienced. Significantly, this transformation tends to consist of a change within the person, such as edification, healing, cleansing or empowerment rather than communal or societal transformation.[4] Once personal transformation has been experienced, it inspires the worshipper into renewed search for God and the process repeats. In this booklet, I will use this framework—search-encounter-transformation—as it relates particularly to a charismatic understanding. However, the process may also be applicable to different spiritual traditions.

A Mothering Model

Sharon Hays's book *Intensive Motherhood* argues that the dominant method of mothering in contemporary Western society is what she terms 'intensive mothering.' Intensive mothering dictates that proper mothering should be 'child-centred, expert-guided, emotionally absorbing, labour-intensive and financially expensive.'[5] Therefore, mothers are expected (and expect of themselves) to give all of their time, energy, love and resources for the proper nurturing and development of their child, who is considered to be innocent, sacred and utterly outside of any market valuation. Hays charts the development of this ideal, showing it to be a modern creation, unknown in our history or in other countries around the world. She also examines how the majority of contemporary childcare manuals uncritically adopt and replicate its assumptions. Her qualitative research shows that whilst not every mother is engaged in intensive mothering, the vast majority assume that this is the correct and best way to parent, such that the best of a mother's love, time, energy, emotions and finances should be endlessly poured into the growing child.

The vast majority assume that intensive mothering is the best way to parent

My conversations with mothers revealed a significant dissonance between Cartledge's worship process expected in church and Hays's mothering model required by society. If women are endlessly to attend to the needs of their child, they are not able also to engage in a search for an encounter with God. Nor indeed are they able to experience that encounter with God which seems to require focused attention—whether through silence or singing or listening or reading—because all of their attention should be upon the needs of their child. The transformative experience thus eludes them because they are not able to follow the proper process to access it. The women I spoke to found a fundamental incompatibility between their assumed mothering duties and their familiar patterns of spirituality. I therefore wanted to find a way to re-conceptualize both worship and motherhood in a biblically faithful way. The following chapters will show how I have sought to do this through the gospel narratives of Mary.

2 Reclaiming Mary our Mother

It was a surprise to discover that Mary could speak meaningfully into this dissonance between contemporary motherhood and worship. This was particularly the case because in my reading on motherhood, Mary continually emerged as the prototype good mother in Christianity. It is arguably the picture of Mary's motherhood as 'gentleness, sweetness, nurturer, patient service and warm refuge' which is in part responsible for generating the intensive mothering stereotypes.[6] She may be a central scriptural figure for any theological understanding of motherhood, but she is often a problematic one because of her idealization.

Before Mary's story can usefully speak to contemporary worshipping mothers, I will demonstrate that she is not, in fact, the good mother as portrayed by tradition. She is, rather, a very ordinary human being and, indeed, ordinary mother, whose example can helpfully critique contemporary notions of intensive mothering described in the previous chapter.[7]

Mary's example can helpfully critique contemporary notions of intensive mothering

First, many of the events in Matthew 1 and Luke 1–2 are hardly the expected appropriate behaviour for a contemporary understanding of an intensive mother. A young, newly pregnant and potentially disgraced girl takes a dangerous solo journey to the hill country to meet Elizabeth (Luke 1.39). Following this, she takes an equally treacherous journey to Bethlehem where she gives birth to her baby surrounded by animals. She places her newborn baby to sleep in an animal feeding trough (Luke 2.7) and welcomes socially disrespected visitors immediately after the birth (Luke 2.16–19). Matthew 2.14 recounts how Mary and Joseph take their child in the middle of the night and flee from Bethlehem to live as refugees in Egypt (Matt 2.13–15). Furthermore, Mary manages to lose her son for three days in the occupied city of Jerusalem (Luke 2.44–46). Each of these scenarios is significantly distanced from the intensive mother aspirations of shielding children from 'the dangerous and corrupt world outside the home.'[8]

In addition to these experiences, the gospels present Mary's motherhood as emotionally complex. Mary is portrayed as jubilant (Luke 1.47), self-giving (Luke 1.38), amazed (Luke 2.33) and treasuring her mothering (Luke 2.19). However, the gospels also record various negative emotions in relation to her mothering. Mary is seen as sorrowful in her motherhood through Simeon's pronouncement to her in the temple (Luke 2.35). In Matthew's gospel, Mary as mother is silenced in the narrative of conception and birth, as Joseph takes the lead (Matt 1.18–25). Upon discovering Jesus in the temple as a boy, Mary is deeply anxious and angry with her son (Luke 2.48), who then rebukes her (2.49). Mary may be seen as embarrassed by Jesus in Mark 3.21–35, where she and her other children think Jesus is out of his mind and try to take hold of him by force. This leads to Jesus appearing to reject them as his true family in Mark 3.33–35. Mary is also portrayed as ignorant of Jesus' mission in John 2.4, where she tries to instigate his first miracle. She is again dismissed by Jesus as misunderstanding him. This diversity of emotions and experiences, contained in a relatively limited number of verses, helpfully critiques the notion that 'good mothers are not vulnerable either to emotional complexity or to moral ambiguity.'[9] Furthermore, Mary's attempts to rebuke Jesus (Luke 2.48), restrain him (Mark 3.21) and override his wishes (John 2.5) do not correlate with intensive mothers who 'use all manner of techniques to avoid spanking or saying no to their children.'[10]

Intensive mothering assumes that non-compliance with the stated techniques will result in less healthy adults, and thus it is this fear which can cause mothers to keep emulating the ideal even whilst resenting it. However, Mary's story demonstrates that complex emotions and experiences in motherhood do not have an automatically detrimental effect upon the child. Whilst I am conscious that it is not possible to draw direct comparisons between Jesus' childhood and the experiences of the rest of humankind, it is enlightening to consider that Mary's mothering experiences intersected with some disturbing and traumatic events, including: social disapproval; homelessness; poverty; genocide; displacement and separation. Matthew presents many of these events as the fulfilment of prophecy; hence they are not simply unfortunate circumstances but they are presented as the intentional way that God planned for Mary's mothering to unfold (Matt 1.23; 2.6; 2.15; 2.17–18). Therefore, whilst intensive mothering advocates that children should be protected at all costs from the corruption of the world, the circumstances in which Mary is called to live out her mothering demonstrate that God may have different priorities.

The woman chosen to be the mother of God's son clearly did not adopt contemporary intensive mothering techniques, but rather lived out her mothering in uncertainty and vulnerability. Mary therefore teaches us that God is not seeking good mothers but faithful disciples, and Jesus makes this clear in Luke 11.27–28:

Mary teaches us that God is not seeking good mothers but faithful disciples

> A woman in the crowd raised her voice and said to him, 'Blessed is the womb that bore you and the breasts that nursed you!' But he said, 'Blessed rather are those who hear the word of God and obey it!'

Here, Jesus is suggesting that God's ultimate call for women is not to motherhood but to hearing the word of God and obeying it. Elizabeth Johnson argues that Jesus is not setting up a contrast between Mary and other disciples through the word 'rather.' She suggests Luke's positive portrayal of Mary as a person of faith means Jesus is agreeing with the blessing the woman pronounces on Mary but is also extending it.[11] Therefore, Jesus can be seen to affirm the value of motherhood whilst also challenging the hearers to understand that although motherhood does develop qualities of love and self-sacrifice in a person, the primary criteria for God's favour are faithfulness and obedience to God's words. The call to 'hear the word of God and obey it' may be summed up as the call to be a disciple. Jesus calls Mary, and indeed every person, to be his disciple, and states that such a call should take precedence even over one's family responsibilities (Luke 14.26; 9.60; Matt 10.34–39).

This pronouncement needs to be set in contrast to contemporary societal models of intensive mothering which suggest that a mother's primary responsibility is to the exclusive nurture and care of her child. Jesus is clear that mothers need first of all to be disciples and worshippers of him. This recognition that God is not calling women to be perfect mothers but rather primarily to be disciples of Jesus has the potential to liberate mothers from oppressive ideals. It can also enable mothers to worship God through their motherhood, rather than seeing their mothering responsibilities as in conflict with their call to worship.

Mary's 'Searching' for God

3

Having suggested that Mary was not a good mother by intensive mothering standards—and is thus able to speak to contemporary mothers in the complexity of their mothering experiences—I will examine the gospel accounts of Mary's life to examine how her experiences of worship might inform the search-encounter-transformation model outlined in chapter one. Obviously, Mary's worship experiences took place in some unique circumstances, and thus are not entirely equivalent to our own. However, in another sense, the uniqueness of her simultaneously worshipful and motherly encounters with God incarnate make her a relevant model for us today. In my conversations with mothers, their most common response to the idea of 'search' in worship was that they were too tired and distracted to engage. This chapter will examine how Mary's experiences can help us to address this challenge.

Worship Through Grace

Mary's pre-eminent encounter with God occurs in the story of the annunciation in Luke 1.26–8. This story significantly critiques the concept of search in that the encounter is not dependent upon Mary's ability to search for it, but upon the gracious election of God. God's initiative is clearly seen in the call of Mary in Luke 1.28. Luke provides the reader with very limited information about Mary before the messenger proclaims God's greeting. Mary is a virgin from Nazareth engaged to be married; thus all that can be assumed is that she is young and of limited means. It is to this peasant girl that a messenger of God declares, 'Greetings, favoured one! The Lord is with you.' Mary is described as being 'much perplexed by his words and pondered what sort of greeting this might be,' which suggests that she did not anticipate or understand such a declaration (Luke 1.29). Therefore it can be assumed that Mary was not in pursuit of such an experience and did not feel deserving of it. Luke is showing that the call of Mary rests wholly on the gracious and unexpected election and initiative of God, rather than on anything particular that Mary had done to 'search' for it. God is both the initiator of Mary's call and the one who makes her able to respond and be considered 'favoured one.'

God's initiative is clearly seen in the call of Mary

When Mary questions how the angel's message is to come true, she is told that 'The Holy Spirit will come upon you, and the power of the Most High will overshadow you,' which further emphasizes the initiative of God (Luke 1.35). Mary is not told she needs to do anything specific in order to bring about this encounter, other than accepting it and making herself available. In her response to God's grace, Luke offers Mary as an ideal disciple in her openness to God's call and as a model for readers to emulate. The story of Mary therefore prompts a re-evaluation of an understanding of search in worship, which places the emphasis upon the worshipper. Mary's experience of encountering God shows that a worshipper's search is not necessary for an encounter to happen, but that God graciously initiates an encounter, and gives the worshipper the grace to respond.

This is not to say that worshippers should never search for an encounter with God; Mary is frequently seen searching for Christ. However, significantly, these searches are often characterized by frustration and rejection, such as the searching for Jesus lost in Jerusalem. A similar experience of searching for Jesus occurs in Mark 3.31–35, which is the only time Mary appears in that gospel. Jesus' mother and brothers come to where he is teaching and call him (Mark 3.31). Jesus responds by saying, 'Who are my mother and my brothers…Whoever does the will of God' (Mark 3.33, 35). The meaning of this passage is brought more to light in Mark 3.21, where Jesus' family is trying to restrain him because of reports they hear that he is out of his mind. Taking these two episodes together, it seems that Mary and the brothers are characterized as not understanding the mission of Jesus and therefore are outside of his eschatological family. This is further emphasized when the scene is combined with the saying in Mark 6.4 where Jesus is not honoured among his own kin. Mary's search for an encounter with Jesus on this occasion resulted not in personal fulfilment, but in failure, rejection, confusion and anger.

Mary is frequently seen searching for Christ

A further occasion where Mary may be seen searching for an encounter with God is when she goes to the temple to present the baby Jesus to God (Luke 2.22). The scene is characterized by rejoicing and amazement, but significantly, there is also a strong recognition of pain and suffering (Luke 2.33). After rejoicing and prophesying about the child Jesus and praising God, Simeon turns his attention to Mary and declares, 'A sword will pierce your own soul too' (Luke 2.35). Traditionally, this violent prophecy was thought to refer to Mary's suffering at seeing Jesus crucified, but Luke does not place Mary at the crucifixion and so does not allow the reader to make this connection. Elizabeth Johnson suggests that it signifies the sword of discernment, following the sword of judgment in Ezek 14.17, and symbolizes Mary's struggle to continue to interpret and remain faithful to the word of God as she has been doing up to this point in the story.[12] Therefore, this soul-piercing is not something unique to Mary. Simeon is acknowledging Mary's painful struggles as mother and disciple as she offers her sacrifice to God within the temple. Therefore, Mary's search for God within the context of worship results in a recognition of pain and confusion as a result of her role, as well as joy and amazement.

These narratives of Mary's searching for divine encounters reveal that, whilst she may expend considerable effort in the search, and occasionally experience positive emotions such as amazement and rejoicing, the result can sometimes be painful and difficult. Whilst the scenes are not exactly comparable to contemporary mothers' experiences of searching for God in worship, Mary's experiences of pain caused by unmet expectations in searching for God resonate with the feelings of anger, neglect, fear and frustration voiced by the mothers to whom I spoke. Searches for God in worship do not always work in the way that we expect or hope. Mary's story offers an important critique of the appropriateness of searching for God with preconceived ideas about what the encounter will be like. Significantly, each of Mary's difficult searches provides the context for fresh understanding: an insight into Jesus' future messiahship in Luke 2.34–35; an affirmation of Jesus' self-identity as God's son in Luke 2.49; and a pronouncement about God's eschatological family in Mark 3.35. Therefore, the difficulties that mothers might experience in worship should not be seen as anomalous or deviant. Rather, they may be a potential means for the worshipping community to learn to encounter God's presence within difficulties.

Mary's story advocates for a focus on God's grace as the foundation for appropriate worship

From Search to Receptivity

Rather than emphasizing search in worship, Mary's story advocates for a focus on God's grace as the foundation for appropriate worship. In addition, when worshippers do search for an encounter with God, this needs to be done without pre-conceived ideas about the nature of that encounter, but rather with an openness to God's initiative which enables greater insight about God's identity and mission. Therefore, I advocate for the reframing of the term 'search' with 'receptivity' in order to convey the openness to God's call which Mary's story exemplifies. Receptivity encompasses search, but also broadens it to recognize that a Christian's primary responsibility in worship is to be receptive to God's gracious initiative as opposed to expending energy searching to orchestrate an encounter with God. Receptivity reminds us that it is God who takes, and has taken, the initiative and not us.

4 Mary's 'Encounters' with God

This chapter examines the nature of Mary's various divine encounters. In many worshipping traditions, the envisaged encounter with God happens most frequently through the stilling of one's mind and heart, for example through sung worship, confession or meditative prayer. Encounter with God often assumes an emptying of oneself in order to be filled by God. For the women I spoke to, the most common response to the encounter stage of the worship process was related to the difficulties they had in switching off their brain in order to enter that place of stillness and self-emptying. In this chapter, I will explore how Mary's stories of encounter with God disrupt these narratives of self-emptying and inner stillness.

Active Encounter

Mary is often assumed to accept her fate passively in Luke 1.38. Her declaration of, 'Let it be with me according to your word' has become the ultimate expression of self-denial and sacrifice and thus has often been seen as a passive self-emptying in response to the divine will. However, the tense of the Greek word *genoito* (let it be with me) is in the aorist tense and the operative mood, which means it expresses a present hope and an expression of joy, desire and longing, which might be best conveyed when translated by the colloquial phrase, 'Bring it on!' Johnson notes that in other biblical stories of divine commissioning, the called do not typically verbalize their consent; the fact that Mary does so here underscores her active, self-assertive role in the events.[13] Scot McKnight describes Mary as 'dangerously active.'[14] Therefore, Mary shows in this scene that encounter with God does not have to be about emptying oneself or switching off but can involve agency, negotiation and active partnership with God.

Mary's declaration might be best translated by the phrase, 'Bring it on!'

Mary's agency is further seen in her encounter with God from the beginning of the annunciation in Luke 1.29. Mary is said to have 'pondered' what sort of greeting the messenger has brought to her (Luke 1.29). The Greek word *dielogizeto* is elsewhere translated in the NRSV as 'questioning' (Luke 3.15; 5.21) and 'discussion' (Luke 20.14). It therefore describes an active, engaged process of discernment, debating and intelligent reasoning. The imperfect tense suggests an ongoing activity that happens throughout this scene. Mary is not just contentedly perplexed or passive; rather, she is involved in critical interpretation of the events unfolding in a way which engages all of who she is rather than emptying it out. This continues in Luke 1.34 when Mary's internal dialogue results in the question, 'How can this be, since I am a virgin?' Significantly, she is not criticized by the angel for engaging her reasoning and questioning mind; rather, she is granted an explanation in v 35 of what will come about if she is willing.

Mary's agency is further seen in her encounter with Jesus in John 2. Mary sees an opportunity for Jesus to begin the ministry that he has been called to and so she takes the initiative to encourage Jesus into action. However, Jesus resists his mother's self-assertive declaration with his refusal to act, saying, 'Woman, what concern is that to you and to me? My hour has not yet come' (John 2.4). Mary seems to be rebuked for the preconceived ideas she has about Jesus in her search for an encounter. However, once the encounter has been initiated, Mary continues to exercise her agency when she says to the servants, 'Do whatever he tells you' and Jesus positively responds to her by acting upon her request (John 2.5). Jesus therefore can be seen here to challenge Mary's active engagement whilst also affirming her.

Charismatic models of worship often encourage worshippers to assert their agency in order to search for an encounter with God, but then to minimize that agency once the encounter has been initiated as they empty themselves in order to be filled by God. The mothers I spoke to had the opposite experience: they did not have the energy to assert their agency in initiating an encounter with God, and when they did engage in an encounter with God they found that they could not empty themselves of their mothering responsibilities. Mary's story challenges both the concept of searching for an encounter with God, and also the impulse to switch off within the divine encounter. Mary continues to exercise her active mind within her divine encounters. Therefore motherly doubts, questions, struggles and tasks which crowd the mind should not be seen as a barrier to encountering God, but rather as potential material for engagement with God.

Motherly doubts, struggles and tasks should be seen as potential material for engagement with God

Furthermore, Mary's encounters with Jesus were not all notable encounters, but were mostly mundane and uneventful, and may therefore critique an understanding that an encounter with God has to be specially felt or experienced. Apart from the story in Luke where the boy Jesus is found in the temple, there is only one verse to describe the majority of Mary's encounters with Jesus: 'They returned to Galilee, to their own town of Nazareth. The child grew and became strong, filled with wisdom; and the favour of God was upon him' (Luke 2.39–40 *cf* 2.52). Behind this verse are years of faithful love, prayer and patient teaching by Mary to the growing Jesus in the context of home and family life. This time is considered to be so marginal that it barely gets a mention in the gospel accounts, and yet without it Jesus would not have been able to do all that followed. The setting for Jesus' childhood, Nazareth, was an inconsequential place, such that Nathanael could ask in John 1.46, 'Can anything good come out of Nazareth?' This further highlights the significant role that Mary would have played in Jesus' experience of love, family life and the enacting of his Jewish traditions. All of this care and nurture took place in Mary's basic domestic sphere within the poor village of Nazareth. Therefore, the vast majority of Mary's encounters with Jesus were at home in basic surroundings, not in well-resourced corporate worship during times of self-emptying.

From Encounter to Recognition

For many worshippers, particularly in a charismatic context, the concept of encounter is enmeshed with an understanding of a felt experience. I therefore suggest that the term 'recognition' is used instead of encounter in conceptualizing appropriate worship. Recognition affirms the exercise of agency on the part of the worshipper in that they must recognize God's presence; it also broadens the focus of divine encounter to include comprehension, rationality and intuition alongside feeling and experiencing. The term 'recognition' conveys an awareness of the gracious initiative of God. It incorporates joyful times of ecstatic encounter, but it can also include times of quiet awareness of God's presence in the ordinary course of life. These recognitions of God's grace and presence can be seen throughout Mary's story as she is frequently characterized as pondering, treasuring and wrestling with what she sees. Therefore, rather than search and encounter, worshipping mothers (and others experiencing alienation from their worshipping traditions) can aspire instead to receptivity and recognition in their worshipping experiences.

Mary's 'Transformations' from God 5

This chapter examines how Mary experienced transformation as a result of her divine encounters. As noted in chapter one, the envisaged transformations which result from an experience of divine encounter can be varied—from therapeutic or physical healing to inner peace or confession or empowerment. However, in each case it is assumed that the transformation leaves the worshipper feeling better off than they were previously, such that the transformation is always positive in some way. For the mothers I interviewed, they found that because they felt unable to engage in search or encounter due to their mothering responsibilities, they were therefore unable to access the desired transformation which they had been accustomed to experiencing as the outcome of worship prior to becoming a mother. This chapter will explore the outcomes of Mary's encounters to show how they were often more ambiguous than the contemporary assumption of a therapeutic transformation.

Mary's spiritual transformation in the story of the annunciation can be seen as a quickly realized and emotionally evidenced positive transformation in line with many charismatic worshippers' expectations. Mary's initial puzzlement at the angel's greeting quickly gives way to her joyful acceptance of God's call in Luke 1.38. Mary is instantly transformed from obscure girl from Nazareth to mother of God's saviour and Elizabeth is the first to recognize and affirm this transformation, as they rejoice together over all that God has done. This scene of jubilation culminates in the Magnificat, where Mary proclaims the permanence of her transformation with the words, 'Surely from now on all generations will call me blessed' (Luke 2.48). Within this scene, there is evidence of a realized transformation resulting from a divine encounter, accompanied by positive emotions. However, this type of transformation is significantly in the minority across the gospel accounts of Mary's life; her experience of a triumphant, realized transformation is soon replaced by uncertainty, pain and worry.

Mary's experience of a triumphant transformation is soon replaced by pain, uncertainty and worry

Struggling Transformation

Following the birth of Jesus and the visit of the shepherds, Mary is again seen pondering God's work in Luke 2.19. The Greek words describing Mary's actions—*sunetērei* (treasured) and *sumballousa* (pondered)—are in the imperfect and present tense respectively. Therefore these verbs describe Mary's ongoing, continuous reasoning as she deeply probes and wrestles with her experiences to discern meaning. Beverly Gaventa characterizes this pondering as worrying, by linking the words used to the Septuagint version of Gen 37.11 where Jacob worries about Joseph's dreams, and Dan 7.28 where Daniel worries about the meaning of an apocalyptic vision.[15] Furthermore, Luke uses *sumballō* in 14.31 to mean 'wage war.' Therefore, Mary's dramatic, jubilant transformation in Luke 1 has turned into a more ongoing process of discernment, wrestling and worry as events have unfolded rather than retaining the stereotypical serene pondering. The various stories of struggled searches for Jesus and difficult encounters with Jesus outlined in previous chapters further portray Mary's inconsistent journey of transforming faith.

This is most clearly seen in Mark 6.4, where Jesus laments the lack of faith in Nazareth and among his family: 'Prophets are not without honour, except in their home town, and among their own kin, and in their own house.' Taken with Mark 3.21–35, it appears that at this point in Jesus' ministry, Mary did not recognize Jesus' messianic identity and mission. Elizabeth Johnson suggests that Mary may not be lacking in faith, but rather actively trying to secure Jesus' safety from hostile groups in order to enable him to fulfil the call she knew he had been given. Johnson argues that Mary may go to Jesus in Mark 3.21 in order 'to persuade her child out of the line of fire' and thus protect the whole family.[16] However, even if this is the case, Jesus' refusal to respond to Mary's efforts shows that Mary had misunderstood his mission. Therefore, even when Mary's encounters with God lead to miraculous and life-altering transformations, most of her faith journey can be seen as a complex and ongoing journey of trying imperfectly to understand and respond to the work of God. This involved both profound experiences of spiritual transformations as well as times of doubt, misunderstanding and anxiety.

Mary's encounters with God involved spiritual transformations as well as misunderstanding and anxiety

Painful Transformation

Mary also experiences pain and agony as an outcome of encounter with Jesus when she appears at the foot of the cross in John 19.25–27. There can be few more painful encounters than conversing with one's son whilst he hangs undeservingly on a cross; therefore the pain of this encounter for Mary cannot be underestimated. Moreover, it is not simply an unfortunate and senseless pain that Mary experiences, but God sovereignly willed this event as part of God's redemption plan. God will not rescue her from the pain of the encounter and transform it with positive feelings. Furthermore, whilst Jesus does offer words of comfort to Mary in committing her to his beloved disciple, this potentially is also a cause of further pain. Jesus does not commit her to her other children, who are perhaps outside of the eschatological family following Mark 3.35. Jesus rather commits her to his beloved disciple, so in being part of the new family of faith Mary must be separated from her natural family. Therefore the transformation of this tragic moment involves a range of negative emotions, which Jesus' actions reinforce rather than mitigate. Transformation is not simply about feeling better. Mary demonstrates that sometimes, the outcome of encounter with Jesus might be to experience further pain and sorrow.

Transformation is not simply about feeling better...it might be to experience further pain

Mary's faith journey offers a great variety of feelings and responses to Jesus. Mary experiences a powerful encounter with God and is transformed into a joyful, amazed prophet, courageously declaring the works of God. However, as her encounters with Jesus continue throughout her life, she also experiences confusion, rejection, worry, doubt, misunderstanding, ambivalence and painful agony which, on each occasion, were not easily or quickly transformed into positive feelings of joy.

It may be argued that Mary experienced such a variety of emotional responses to Jesus because she did not yet have the full revelation of Jesus' identity and mission that comes through the resurrection. Mary's responses to Jesus were often the wrong ones because she did not fully understand what he came to do, whereas, post-resurrection, Mary is seen among the faithful disciples awaiting the gift of the Holy Spirit in Jerusalem in Acts 1.14. However, even if this portrait is Luke's intention, it is discordant with the experiences of the mothers I spoke to. These mothers are Spirit-filled believers who relate to Jesus through the resurrection; however, they continue to experience a range of varied responses to their encounters with God analogous with Mary's, and thus suggest that Mary's experiences were not unique.

From Transformation to Response

Mary shows that there is not one homogenous, positive outcome to encounter with God, but a variety of ways to respond. Therefore I advocate for broadening the concept of transformation into response. Responses can include a positive, uplifting transformation of feeling as a valid outcome of recognizing God, but also allow for a variety of other outcomes, which might not always be positive. Affirming a variety of responses to encounter with / recognitions of God can enable those who presently feel excluded from worship to appreciate the validity of their recognitions, and resist dismissing them as not proper because they do not result in the expected therapeutic transformation.

6 Learning to Sing Mary's Song

As we have seen, Mary was *receptive* to God's initiative, *recognized* God at work and *responded* with faithfulness. Her experiences thus challenge and broaden the search-encounter-transformation model common in contemporary understandings of worship. Mary's receptivity-recognition-response model has the potential to affirm more varied experiences of worship than the charismatic search-encounter-transformation model has often envisaged. In this final chapter, I shall examine Mary's Magnificat as the manifesto of her approach to worship to see what final lessons Mary has to share. This chapter will be particularly focused on the implications of the Magnificat for charismatic worship practices (as described in the various booklets listed in footnote 2).

First, following on from the previous chapter, it is apparent that the setting of the Magnificat shows that Mary's song is offered as a *response* to God's gracious initiative, rather than as a means of searching for a divine encounter. This further reinforces the discussions in chapter three that argue that search should be reinterpreted as receptivity to God's gracious activity. Charismatic sung worship may have an unhelpful tendency unwittingly to subvert this dynamic so that the songs become the expected mechanism for experiencing God's grace, rather than a means of responding to it. The positioning of the Magnificat as a response to God provides an important corrective to this tendency.

Mary's song is a response to God's initiative, rather than a search for a divine encounter

Not only does the positioning support a focus on the initiative of God, but also the content of the hymn consistently foregrounds the work of God. Every clause in the hymn apart from the first is about what God has done: (God) has looked with favour; the mighty one has done great things; (God) has shown strength; (God) has scattered; (God) has brought down; (God) has filled; (God) has helped (Luke 1.46–47). Mary's activities of magnifying and rejoicing in Luke 1.46–47 receive little attention and serve to convey her response to God's initiative rather than seeing her activity as in some way necessary to the transformation she has experienced. This sustained focus on the activity and initiative of God critiques the common tendency in charismatic songs to focus overly on the efforts and activities of the worshippers or the transformative outcomes of worshipping God.

Furthermore, whilst there is a clear sense of joy in the act of singing, 'My spirit rejoices in God my saviour', it is a joy which is 'written against the whole canvas of the world's pain' (Luke 1.47).[17] Mary's joy is not an escape from life's difficulties but is rather a living in the midst of them; she is trusting God to bring salvation through the reversal of traditional structures of power and privilege. Mary's joy was not just for herself but was for all who would benefit from this reversal of world systems. Mary's song is therefore far removed from an individual emotional high or positive personal transformation in singing; it is rather a joyful response to God's initiative in solidarity with all who are oppressed.

Mary's joy is not an escape from life's difficulties but is rather a living in the midst of them

Mary's status as a lowly servant further emphasizes her solidarity with the downcast on whose behalf she rejoices (Luke 1.48). Mary calls herself *doulos*, meaning slave, and her declaration of lowliness connects her with Hagar (Gen 16.11) and the enslaved Hebrews of Egypt (Exod 3.7). Mary can boldly and joyfully declare herself to be a persecuted, rejected and oppressed slave because she understands that this is precisely the reason why God chose her—it was because of her lowly socio-economic position that she was called, and not in spite of it. The song speaks explicitly against the rich, the rulers and the proud, those who are characteristically the ones most able to assert themselves. In contrast, Mary declares that God looks with favour on the lowly, lifting them up and filling them with good things. Mary rejoices in her identification with the downcast whom God's activities will benefit. This focus on lowliness further critiques an emphasis on the worshipper's initiative in the encounter, and also significantly challenges any contemporary charismatic culture that is accidentally celebrating its middle-class comforts rather than joining in with the Magnificat's renunciations of wealth and power.

Mary's song moves from what God has done for her in the here and now to what God has done and will do for all people throughout history. The song begins in the first person (my soul, my spirit, my saviour, great things for me) and then moves into the plural, so that Mary's individual experience has profound implications for other people, and this is the cause of her celebration. This opening up of the work of God from the individual to the global critiques the tendency in contemporary worship songs to focus further in upon the here and now and the transformed feelings of the gathered worshippers rather than singing about the global and universal activity of God. Thus, sung worship can be seen as unhelpfully exclusive in contrast to the radical inclusivity of Mary's hymn of praise.

This theme of inclusivity and social justice is powerfully expressed by Mary as a reordering of the world's priorities. The song moves from her own experiences of God to God's mighty dealings with the whole world. For Mary, God has brought down the proud, powerful and rich of the world and lifted up the lowly and hungry and thus God desires to include those who are traditionally excluded in society. Therefore, if God's purpose is to include the excluded, this offers a significant critique to much contemporary worship, which often excludes those unable to participate due to their circumstances.

The mothers I spoke to often felt excluded from the act of worship within their charismatic tradition. Their experiences expose deficiencies in models of worship that expect people to expend effort in a search to engage in a divine encounter of self-emptying in order to feel a positive transformation. The mothers' experiences of exclusion raise the question of who else might be excluded from similar worshipping models because of their circumstances. It is not just mothers who may be unable to assert their effort in searching for an encounter with God, or who may find the focus on positively transformed feelings to be unsuccessful. Fathers of young children may have similar experiences when they share in childcare. Likewise, those who suffer tiredness and distraction due to illness, other caring responsibilities, mental illness or old age may also struggle to participate. Each of these groups may be similarly excluded from the act of contemporary sung worship. Mary's prophetic declarations of God's enduring commitment to the excluded therefore offer a significant challenge to the church to renew its worship in order to rectify the experiences of alienation that many may encounter.

Mary does not just sing the Magnificat but embodies its hope

Furthermore, learning to sing Mary's song is not just about incorporating the themes of the Magnificat into our singing repertoire, but also allowing her story to readdress and redefine the contemporary models of motherhood that we inhabit. Mary does not just sing the Magnificat but embodies its hope. She is one of the lowly who has been exalted by God and so she has experienced the reordering of the world's priorities that she sings about. The Magnificat challenges not just methods of worshipping God, but a whole way of life. If worship is to be orientated to God's initiatives of social justice and inclusivity, worshippers similarly need to embody the good news which they sing about, and thus find ways daily to live out God's radical agenda. One cannot joyfully sing about bringing down the powerful and lifting up the lowly if we are not similarly living out this radical vision in our own lives. Mary demonstrates that worshipping God is not just a case of singing songs about social justice in response to God's initiative during times of worship; it is a whole way of life seeking to embody God's radical agenda of inclusivity.

Finally, despite these critiques of contemporary charismatic worship, the Magnificat also affirms the place for Holy Spirit-inspired singing as a legitimate means of expressing worship and praise to God. Significantly, sung worship is not the only or best way to offer worship to God but it is a means of uniquely expressing passion, commitment and joy to God in response to God's gracious initiative. Mary challenges us that the solution to the present challenges with contemporary sung worship is not to dismiss it entirely, but rather to channel it appropriately as one part of a whole life worshipping God in a rich variety of ways.

7 Conclusion

This booklet set out to show how Mary can be reclaimed as a discipleship role model for contemporary mothers struggling to relate their spirituality to their motherhood. The research underpinning this booklet was carried out in a charismatic-church context and so many of the observations relate specifically to a contemporary worshipping culture. However, I have tried to show that many of the insights similarly relate to other worshipping traditions, and indeed perhaps to groups of people other than mothers.

I have argued for a redefinition of the three themes that inform the worship process of search, encounter, and transformation in order to reduce the dissonance worshipping mothers experience. Mary's story enables these concepts to be broadened, so that worship of God is conceptualized instead in terms of receptivity, recognition and response. The term 'receptivity' is more helpful than 'search' because it may incorporate the activity of searching for an encounter with God, such as at the wedding at Cana, but it foregrounds the gracious initiative of God, who responds to requests, but also challenges assumptions. Receptivity conveys an openness to encountering God in a variety of ways rather than approaching worship with preconceived ideas about the form that encounter will take. Likewise, the term 'recognition' is a more holistic way to conceive of encounters because it may include a felt, self-offering encounter with God, such as the annunciation, but it focuses more upon the exercise of personal agency in the ongoing apprehension of God in the context of ordinary life. Finally, 'response' is a more inclusive way of understanding transformation because responses may encompass an experience of singing which produces positive feelings of joy and awe—such as the Magnificat—but more importantly, it highlights the ongoing journey of faith. A focus on responses affirms the possibility of a variety of outcomes to worship, which may involve pain, doubt and struggle as well as joy.

True worship should be orientated towards recognition of the grace of God

The analysis of the Magnificat affirms the appropriate focus on God's initiative within a sung worship response. It highlights the significance of inclusivity, both for the sung worship encounter itself, but also for the whole of life. It affirms that worship is not just a one-off event, but rather, true worship should be orientated towards ongoing receptivity and recognition of the grace of God. Therefore, like the search-encounter-transformation worship model, receptivity, recognition, response is also a cyclical process in which worship is a feature of daily discipleship where our responses to God enable our ongoing receptivity to God's initiative.

So what can churches do to help remove the dissonance that mothers experience in their worship? First, the intensive mother ideal is not a helpful, realistic or theologically defensible way to conceptualize motherhood, and therefore churches need to spend time theologically reflecting upon the concept of mother (and also probably father or parent). This could involve asking questions such as: what is the role of a mother? What is distinctive about a Christian mother? How can the church enable women better to fulfil this role? Further work needs to be done at an academic level in order to provide churches with the necessary resources, but a first step is for churches to realize that this is a vital issue with which to engage. Individual churches have responsibility to reflect upon the ways in which their practices might be unintentionally reinforcing the mother stereotypes. Issues such as: the layout of the worshipping space; the creche provisions; the explicit and implicit attitudes to baby noise; the location of the toys and changing facilities; the timings and content of the services—all these affect mothers' experience of church and reinforce expected behaviour of mothers in church. These experiences and behaviours come to inform their perceptions of worship and God, and thus the practices need to be reinforcing a right understanding.

Churches need to spend time theologically reflecting upon the concept of mother

In addition, it is not just churches who have a responsibility to redefine motherhood. The mothers themselves were found to be adherents of the ideal through the way they had internalized the intensive mother script, even whilst resenting it. Therefore, women need to find ways to empower themselves and one another to resist the oppressive concept in their lives. This may be achieved first by recognizing the concept and becoming aware of how it influences their experiences. Secondly, this awakening needs to be shared with other people since the strength to resist and redefine the ideals needs to come from solidarity with others. This goes beyond groups of mothers supporting each other courageously to redefine their mothering. It is vital that a critical mass of other people in their social sphere affirm and champion such redefinitions in order to subvert perceptions of deviance in relation to those who do not conform to the ideals. Churches are ideally situated to provide the necessary community for such a countercultural revolution. Talking, praying and reflecting together as a church on these issues are vital ways of starting such a revolution that can bring liberation to all contemporary mothers struggling with the ideal models, not just those in charismatic churches.

Secondly, the experiences of alienation from worship which the mothers relate have exposed how particular models of worship can tend to be non-inclusive. Whilst the experience of early motherhood may be unique, the symptoms which prompt the alienation are not. These symptoms may include: tiredness; mental and emotional overload; an unpredictable relationship with time; physiological changes; and demanding responsibilities. Such issues may affect many other groups of people and similarly cause them to feel alienated from worship. Such groups may include: other carers; the elderly; those with mental health issues; the disabled; and those who work shifts, to name but a few. The analysis of the Magnificat highlighted the importance of inclusivity in God's agenda. That various groups of people may be experiencing alienation from worship should prompt a reimagining of personal and corporate worship as an urgent matter of social justice.

These suggestions have important implications for ministers, worship leaders and song writers, highlighting the need for all such ministers to have theological training to ensure that songs are produced, and worship is led, in a responsible and theologically informed way. In addition, it is not just worship leaders who are shaping the theological narrative of a worship service. Any service leader, intercessor or preacher contributes to the informal liturgy which shapes the way worship is conceptualized and experienced, so there is perhaps more work to do in training and reflection on what it is we do when we gather to worship and how this informs our day-to-day spirituality.

Thirdly, we can see the important role that Mary can play in discussions about worship. Protestants have tended to avoid talking about Mary; however, this booklet has shown that Mary has much to say to the contemporary church about worship, particularly in a charismatic context. Mary's experiences of encounter with God, her prophetic song, and her ongoing journey of discipleship all contain rich insights that the Protestant church is missing out on through its avoidance of her. Therefore, I urge charismatics to re-engage with Mary, and allow her to inform their theology of worship. This can be done through a sermon series or small group study, dramatization and art, or creative use of the Magnificat outside of Evensong.

Mary has much to say to the contemporary church about worship

Mary often feels inaccessible to many contemporary Christians and is rarely a spiritual resource for mothers within Protestant churches, despite the rich material she provides. Hopefully this booklet will inspire people to reclaim Mary as our mother, one who struggled with the complex demands of raising a family and imperfectly tried to balance this with her committed discipleship journey. Would that a new generation of Christian mothers might be inspired by Mary to resist society's oppressive stereotypes of mother and their churches' narrow understandings of worship, and pioneer ways faithfully to inhabit the primary invitation to discipleship to which Jesus calls us all.

Notes

1 H Collins, 'Weaving a Web: Developing a Feminist Practical Theology Methodology from a Charismatic Perspective' in N Slee, F Porter and A Phillips (eds), *Researching Female Faith: Qualitative Research Methods* (Abingdon: Routledge, 2018) p 54.

2 Unpublished PhD thesis, H Collins, *Weaving Worship and Womb: A Feminist Practical Theology of Charismatic Worship from the Perspective of Early Motherhood* (University of Bristol, 2017).

3 I do not have the space here to define the charismatic movement beyond how it relates to the process of spirituality described. There are a number of useful Grove booklets which address issues of definitions and characteristics: C Buchanan, *Encountering Charismatic Worship* (Grove Worship booklet W51); V Cooke, *Understanding Songs in Renewal* (Grove Renewal booklet R4); M Bonnington, *Patterns in Charismatic Spirituality* (Grove Renewal booklet R28); J Leach, *Renewing Charismatic Worship* (Grove Renewal booklet R37); N Drake, *A Deeper Note: The 'Informal' Theology of Contemporary Sung Worship* (Grove Worship booklet W218).

4 M Cartledge, *Encountering the Spirit: The Charismatic Tradition,* (London: Darton, Longman and Todd, 2006) p 26.

5 S Hays, *The Cultural Contradictions of Motherhood* (New Haven, CT: Yale University Press, 1996) p 8. See also L R Ennis (ed), *Intensive Mothering: The Cultural Contradictions of Modern Motherhood,* (Toronto: Demeter Press, 2014) for an updated discussion of intensive mothering.

6 J van den Hengel, 'Miriam of Nazareth: Between Symbol and History' in Amy-Jill Levine (ed), *A Feminist Companion to Mariology* (London: T and T Clark, 2005) p 137.

7 E Storkey, 'The Significance of Mary for Feminist Theology' in D Wright (ed), *Chosen by God: Mary in Evangelical Perspective* (London: Marshall, Morgan and Scott Publications Ltd, 1989) p 196.

8 S Hays, *op cit,* p 124.

9 P Cooey, '"Ordinary Mother" as Oxymoron: The Collusion of Theology, Theory and Politics in the Understanding of Mothers' in J Hanigsberg and S Ruddick (eds), *Mother Troubles: Rethinking Contemporary Maternal Dilemmas* (Boston, MA: Beacon Press, 1999) p 238.

10 S Hays, *op cit,* p 116.

11 E Johnson, *Truly Our Sister: A Theology of Mary in the Communion of Saints* (London: Continuum, 2003) p 247.

12 *ibid,* p 281.

13 *ibid,* p 254.

14 S McKnight, *The Real Mary: Why Evangelical Christians Can Embrace the Mother of Jesus* (London: SPCK, 2007) p 26.

15 B Gaventa, 'All Generations Will Call Me Blessed: Mary in Biblical and Ecumenical Perspective' in A-J Levine (ed), *A Feminist Companion to Mariology* (London: T and T Clark, 2005) p 127.

16 E Johnson, *op cit,* p 221.

17 E Johnson, *op cit,* p 265.